THE LADY WITH THE POOL

THE
LADY
WITH THE
POOL

APRIL BAKER

To protect the privacy of individuals featured,
all names in this story have been changed.

The Lady with the Pool
Copyright © April Baker

The right of April Baker to be identified as the author of this work has been asserted by her in accordance with the Copyright, Designs and Patents Act 1988.

First published in 2023

All rights reserved. No part of this publication may be reproduced or transmitted in any form or by any means, electronic or mechanical, including photocopying, recording, or any information storage and retrieval system without permission in writing from the author.

British Library Cataloguing Data
A catalogue record of this book is available from The British Library

Published for April Baker by Verité CM Ltd

ISBN: 978-1-914388-39-2

Cover design and layout by Abi Hood

Edited by Helen Johnson

Printed in England

"Weebles wobble but they don't fall down"

Acknowledgements

To my family
Thank you for being gracious in allowing me to write my story which essentially is yours too. I love each one of you; with all my heart.

To the three people who encouraged me to write my story long before I thought it even possible. I will be forever grateful.

To my amazing God who planted this idea, planned it from the beginning and will use it to do exactly as You wish. Life is such an adventure with You, I don't know why anyone would do life without you.

To my reader
I hope and pray my story brings hope, strength and ultimately draws you further into your true identity.

One

Having a wobble!

Have you ever been misunderstood, misrepresented or perceived in such a way that it shakes you? Or have you been described by the stuff you own as if that is the most interesting thing about you? Well if the answer is yes, you and I have something in common.

When I said "shakes you" I would like to explain. A good friend once called me a Weeble. These were toy characters that were in a weighted egg-shape back in the 1970's. When they were tipped and they hit the ground they would wobble around until gravity brought them back to the upright position. The advert used to say "Weebles wobble but they don't fall down".

Well over the years I have wobbled, many times, BUT I didn't fall down.

The battle is to not fall down when our identity is knocked, or circumstances unsettle us.

I think when people say things about us that rock our identity, or aren't true about us, we have a choice and if we don't make that choice quickly, the hurt will decide for us.

We need to choose to stand firm in who we are. I really don't say this lightly as many people don't know who they are. So right now I'm encouraging you to find out before such a thing takes place.

You see I've had a few mountains to climb, battles to fight and hurdles to jump (and every other annoying analogy of difficulties). Life has been hard; in the matters of the heart, every day life, in health and relationships.

I am, however, materially very blessed. I have a very lovely home, a car to drive, a swimming pool and a hot tub, food to eat and nice clothes to wear. I'm not telling you this to boast but to help you understand that things from other peoples' perspective can look very rosy for me.

I've had a lady from our village talk about me. She has told others that I "drive around in my big car, and live in my big house thinking I'm better than everyone else". When I heard this I was horrified. I would never want anyone to think that I look down on them, and in reality I really don't. I am so aware that we are all created equal before God. He loves each one of us as His kids; whether we acknowledge that or not.

I have spent time with boys that are street kids in Narok Kenya, girls who have escaped FGM and early forced marriage and women that didn't manage to escape. I have sat with women who work in the sex industry and many I would consider my friends, but this person did not know that, and she doesn't know my heart.

One particular day my husband was cutting the grass in our field that extends behind her house. It was the middle of summer and he had worked a long day but knew he still needed to mow the field. It was around 9.30pm and he got on his tractor and began the task.

In the countryside farmers work all hours especially during harvest so he did not think this unusual.

Around 10pm I heard very loud knocking. I got up as was already in bed and went to find out what was going on. I found this neighbour at our front door.

We had lived there around 10 years and had never used this door as it comes into our dining room and was creaky, old and not near the driveway.

I opened the window and asked her if I could help. She screamed a barrage of abuse at me about how we were selfish and thoughtless for working so late at night and what horrible people we were. I apologised for the disturbance but didn't manage to get too many words out as I was so upset at the things she was calling me. I went and asked my husband to stop and then cried. This was quite a "wobble".

I was sat on my bed crying when I heard the Lord say in my heart "what door did she go to?" I was really confused at first, thinking what on earth has that got to do with anything and then He answered "She used the front door, no one who KNOWS you goes to that door - SHE DOESN'T KNOW YOU".

I knew in that moment, despite feeling sick to my stomach, that she didn't know me and that it didn't matter what she thought of me. God did know me and He did know my heart.

Don't get me wrong there was still a big part of me that didn't want her to misunderstand me, but in the end I could stop from "falling down" because I knew God could see me and looked at my heart.

In knowing <u>whose</u> we are and knowing <u>who</u> we are, can make such a difference. In fact, it makes all the difference.

Our true identity is found when we let go of what other people have made us feel like, what ideas we have of ourselves and in allowing God to show us who He has created us to be. It is a journey worth taking. This is where you find freedom to be the real you.

In another situation I was at a Christian event and I was helping tidy up with a Christian friend. I know him really well. He is an awesome man of God who ministers to people all the time and is a lot of fun to be around.

A man unfamiliar to either of us was assisting. He asked my friend how he was involved in the charity and what he did for a living. After he had given examples of how God was using him, the man turned to me and said "what about you?" Before I could even answer my friend said "Oh, she's the lady with the pool".

Now don't misunderstand me I'm sure my friend didn't mean anything by this. I however was very upset. I had been described by possessions I had, as if that was the most outstanding thing about me. It hurt and I wanted to justify who I was, not what I had. Instead, in that moment, I chose to laugh and hide my true feelings and not react too strongly. This book title however concludes it could have been a defining moment for me.

I think deep down each of us has a desire to be known. To be fully understood. For our heart to be heard and accepted. Even our love for others' to be acknowledged, or our generosity to be noted - symbols of who we are in our hearts and not by our worldly achievements.

I believe we are created in the likeness of God, and He looks at the heart. Therefore, we want our hearts to be understood, as it is the very essence of what makes us unique. None of us are replicas but individual works of art; originals.

The real you is found in stripping back the canvas and finding the original painting underneath the doodles and scrawling's that our experiences and other people have placed on top. It may be that hurt and disappointment has even led you to deface your own identity. Each of our canvas' need cleaning up and restoring.

It's when we live out of who we have been created to be and not what this world has moulded us to become, that we discover our true self; our original design, the masterpiece.

I heard the other day someone say that we all want to

know: where we have come from, what our purpose is here, and where we are going after.

I agree 100%. When you feel confident in knowing the answers to these questions you know you won't fall, even if you occasionally still wobble.

Two

Going back to the very beginning

In the search to understand our identity we look to our "story" - where we are from and how we have got to be where we are.

Having worked with many young people in Care and Careleavers, I've seen how this desire can become all consuming.

When asked the question "where are you from?" people often respond with the place in which they were born, or the country their family have originated from. This seeks to identify us within a community.

I was born in Nottinghamshire to a working class family. My father worked hard having studied mechanical engineering and progressed into computer programming and maintenance. My mother took care of my older sister and I, only really working outside the home when we were a bit older.

I came into the world with a bit of a battle, not that I remember it of course. I am told that I was delivered feet first with the umbilical cord wrapped around my neck; my brain starved of oxygen for a while. At the time this caused great concern. (My dad always joked years later that it explained a lot!)

My family moved to Suffolk when I was 3 years old as my father got a better paid job. It is around this time that I began bumping into things and not responding quite as would be expected. It was discovered that I had very poor eyesight which was soon adjusted with the help of glasses.

My mother was very loving and often had a smile and made us laugh. She taught my sister and I how to do things in the home and encouraged us in our schooling.

My father loved to cuddle us and could be a lot of fun. He was however very strict. His parenting style was one that demanded respect, and fear was the motivator.

I remember overstepping the mark on a handful of occasions that led to a handprint being left on the back of my legs.

I have since found out that he used a watered-down parenting style from the one he had encountered. I believe his mother was a force to be reckoned with.

My father reaped a lot worse as a child than I did, which as an adult helped me to understand his temper and discipline.

On one occasion, my Dad had been naughty at school and my grandmother had been called by the headmaster. She was so angry with him that she made him crawl on hands and knees, while she kicked him, all the way home.

By the time I met my grandmother she already had dementia.

My fathers' parents lived in a two up-two down terraced house. It had a front room only to be used on "special occasions". In my lifetime I never knew it to actually be used.

The back room was the kitchen, sitting room and dining room all in one and was very small. Outside was the outhouse with the high level pull chain toilet. This building terrified me. It was freezing cold, full of spiders, dark and smelled of sewers.

At the end of the street there was an old fashioned corner shop that sold sweets individually. When we visited, my Nan would give my older sister and I some pennies to go and buy some. She would often say to my sister "Here take this, I'm giving you more money than your sister as I prefer you".

She didn't hide this from me and would say it right in front of me. My sister kindly always shared the money equally as soon as we were out the door. My Nan's temper had softened with age and her grandchildren never saw that side of her.

When I was 7 years old I became very poorly with whooping cough, croup and flu. The local doctor visited me daily at home checking on my progress. My mum attentively nursed me but the recovery was slow. I think my parents had been worried that I might not survive.

I attended primary school in the village where we lived. I liked to study and found that if I did well it really pleased my Dad. With any achievement, he would always push me that bit harder, which I think led me to strive for perfection.

Wanting to do well is good. However, if left unchecked perfectionism can be self-obsessing and can even be destructive. The pursuit of doing your best, in everything, all the time, and never being satisfied doesn't lead to happiness. This is something I wrestled with until I found freedom from it. We will get to that later!

One day a lady from the village told my parents that the village church had a Sunday School and that my sister and I would enjoy it. In the desire to entertain us and have Sunday mornings to themselves, my parents signed us up. Here I first learnt stories of Jesus and heard of God.

The message I picked up was of a holy God who hates our sin, our imperfection, but wants to make us perfect. The striving for perfection only accelerated.

Attending Middle School was quite a different experience from the lovely friendly primary school I had enjoyed. Girls aged 9 to 12 years can be so fickle and unkind. I had friends some days and on other days the very same girls would hate me and bully me. The desire to be understood, accepted and heard seemed to grow with each rejection. I tried using humour and being a bit naughty to gain peer acceptance.

We had a teacher called Mrs Sprice. On her first day she introduced herself and shouted at us that she would only accept "Manners and Sensibility". She repeated this statement about 5 times and then wrote a large M and a large S on the chalk board. She shouted at me "You girl, what does M and S stand for?" I replied "Marks & Spencer's". The whole class fell about laughing. I was sent out of the room.

Getting in trouble at school, while trying to ensure my work was perfect all of the time, and having a very strict father was a big balancing act. One that often worked against each other.

In 1984, my parents were invited to accompany my sister and I to a football stadium to hear an American Evangelist called Billy Graham. They both came. It was this evening that both my parents heard that God loved them and wanted them to return to Him. God wanted to forgive them for all that they had done wrong and because of Jesus they could have peace with God. They gave their lives to Jesus. This was the beginning of great change for my family.

My family joined a chapel in the next village and it became our extended family. My dad became very strict about not doing anything on a Sunday to dishonour God. It was too restrictive but he softened in time.

One weekend my family had invited a lot of the congregation to a barbecue.

I recall that my dad said something to me and I answered him back in a way he didn't like. He responded in haste, hitting me and I stumbled and fell to the floor. I knew by the look in his eyes he was furious. I got up and ran upstairs locking myself in the bathroom, scared of what was going to happen next.

My father banged and banged on the door, demanding I opened it. When I refused he started breaking in. I could hear my mum and my sister crying and then the voice of a lady from church.

I can't remember if I let them in or if he broke in but I do remember my dad shouting at me that I had embarrassed him. He implied I had thrown myself to the floor for dramatic effect and to make him look bad. Due to having an audience he then left.

The lady from the church proceeded to comfort me, and then suggested that he would never have done that to my sister as he obviously preferred her.

This reoccurring theme played on my mind for many years. Did everyone prefer my sister to me? Why didn't they like me as much?

In the years that followed I attended many Christian groups for young people and really learned about God and how His Son loved me so much.

I started talking to Him and hearing Him talk to me in a still small voice within.

Our chapel got a new young pastor who was newly married. It was exciting and I loved spending time with them, learning all I could from them.

A young family also joined from America, he was in the United States Airforce. Our friendship became one that was unrivalled. (They have had such an impact on my life). They showed Jesus to me, in who they were and how they lived.

More and more families from the surrounding villages started to come along to the church and there was a real sense of community and family. I found acceptance and belonging there.

This sense of security was suddenly shaken when I found out that someone close to me in age was having an inappropriate relationship with the pastor I looked up to. I was devastated. How could this be? Was this all just a big lie?

The pastor and his wife had a young son and I often took care of him. His wife took this revelation very deeply. Her response was of anger and wanted the young girl to pay for what she had done. I could see her hurt but even as a teenager

I couldn't comprehend why she was dealing with it in the way that she was.

This wobble really made me re-evaluate my beliefs. I came to the conclusion that I still loved God but I wasn't so sure I liked His people.

It was here that I also determined within myself that if I ever got married that I would never ever cheat. I had seen all the hurt and pain it had caused and I hated it. I also decided that if anyone ever cheated on me I would never deal with it in the same way the pastors' wife had either. (Sadly this decision was tested later in my life).

I had been shaken by all of this, but I did not stay down. I had gotten up again, stronger in my convictions. However, my feelings of acceptance and belonging to this community now felt tainted. I wasn't sure I wanted it as much as I had before. I knew they couldn't be relied upon the way I had once thought. This sadness didn't shift easily.

I spent more time with friends who didn't profess to know Jesus as I felt they couldn't hurt me as much.

As my GCSE exams loomed, the pressure for perfection grew and grew. I worked hard but also felt overwhelmed by it all. I did manage to get 10 qualifications; resulting in 1 A and 9 B's.

I remember phoning my parents to tell them. My mum was delighted. My Dad asked what I got the A in and said "what was wrong with the other subjects?"

When my older sister had received her results two years previously she had attained a mixture of grades from A to D. Dad had seemed pleased with her and congratulated her.

This reinforced the belief that he preferred her to me.

Years later my sister told me she had been upset about it too. She had thought that Dad always treated me like I could achieve more than her and assumed I was the clever one. It's so strange how we all see the same situation so very differently.

The summer after my exams, I spent staying at my friend Gemma's house. She had two older brothers and she had a pool. Her brothers would take us clubbing and their mates would supply us with alcohol. I didn't expect as much from these people so felt less likely to get hurt.

I ended up dating one of the older brothers' mates. He was a lot older than me.

The evening he asked me to be his girlfriend I remember replying "You won't want to date me I don't believe in sex before marriage and I won't marry you". He laughed and said that he admired my straightforward speaking and did want to date me anyway.

He was kind to me and made me feel good about myself.

I started Sixth Form with the intent of becoming a Barrister. I studied Politics, Economics, Maths and Further Maths. I joined the Oxbridge club and wanted to go to Oxford University.

The school play this particular year was to be Blood Brothers and I got the main part as the leading lady.

I also ran for Head Girl.

My picture of perfection was coming to pass and yet I still felt dissatisfied with myself.

At Christmas time I went shopping with my boyfriend to Norwich. We went into Top Shop and I remember feeling like the world was spinning faster and faster. I collapsed and had to be carried back to the car. I suffered with a flu-like illness over the festive period with a high fever and at times was delusional.

By the January I was feeling worse and worse. I had a rash that covered my torso and immense pain in my joints and back.

As each week past I was getting further and further behind in my studies. The stress was awful. How would I ever catch up?

Doctors were really unsure what was wrong. The illness

progressed until I couldn't walk and I spent many weeks in hospital. I couldn't keep much food down and my body weight nearly halved.

I spent most days in bed and only found a little enjoyment in life, outside of my relationships, through new crafts and day time television.

I spent a lot of time alone. My mum now had a full time job and my sister was studying foundation level art. I think they both spent as much time with me as they possibly could, some days even missing work and college.

(This time of my life is quite vague from the many different medications I had for the intense pain. This resulted in me sleeping quite a lot.)

I had to withdraw from school because by this point I was too far behind. I felt it was out of my control and that I was failing.

On one occasion I was in hospital, and due to muscle spasms, I couldn't move my arms or legs. I was on morphine for pain control and was attempting to sleep. The medication made me hallucinate that my body was crawling with spiders. It was horrible.

I was on a bay with elderly ladies who all had dementia.

One night I was awoken as a lady had placed her hand over my face demanding I give her stolen handbag back. I screamed and screamed until the nurses came running. This did not aid my recovery or help me get any sleep!

In the months ahead I had to learn to walk again and build my muscle strength very slowly.

One well-meaning Christian said I shouldn't wonder why any of this had happened to me. She said that there were so many people in the world suffering from one thing or another, that really I should ask "why not me"?

This meant that I fully embraced the illness for a while and almost saw it as my God-given "lot" in life.

My boyfriend stayed around visiting me daily. Most of my friends were brilliant at the beginning but soon fell away as time past.

Day to day I spent many hours on my own. I knew God was with me and I felt His presence.

The unrelenting pain and the uncertainty of how long it would last was a very lonely place.

There was one particular day I remember thinking that if my health didn't improve, having lost most of my friends, and even if my family deserted me, that I knew I would be okay.

I knew I had strength from God and my ultimate reliance was upon Him. It wasn't a comfortable position I was in but it was a defining one.

In the Bible, Paul speaks about knowing how to be content in all situations and I think I had found it. Contentment needed defining though, as I certainly didn't want to stay in that place!

I started to know deep within myself that God was saying He wanted me well. I really think this was the beginning of my recovery from what now had been a three year illness.

Recovery wasn't overnight but I got better and better.

Having elaborated on my first nineteen years' and telling this part of my story, I could consider that I have answered the question of where I am from. If I believed this to be all there was however, I would see myself with a clouded view.

My summary could have been that I was from a typical 2.4 English family, always second best to my sister, a sickly person and a perfectionist who never quite achieved perfection.

In the years that followed these formative experiences, I discovered that if I allowed them to, I could let these beliefs define me. In doing so I would have been selling myself short and would have been held back from my true identity.

You see I started my story on the day of my birth but that

is not going back to the very beginning. Long before I was even a twinkle in my parents' eye, God had a purpose and a plan for me.

"Before I formed you I knew you"

Jeremiah 1:5

I was known before I was even born. My deep longing to be known and to be understood had already been met long before I even arrived. So, I am "from" God. This is my origin. It's so hard to comprehend but so exciting and reassuring a journey.

"And in love he chose us before he laid the foundation of the universe! Because of his great love, he ordained us, so that we would be seen as holy in his eyes with an unstained innocence."

Ephesians 1:4 TPT

The concept that I have been chosen by God, out of love, certainly makes the feeling of being second best fade. I am accepted by Him!

As I consistently dwelt on that truth, over time that became more dominant.

Being seen as pure and innocent also takes the momentum of perfectionism away. If Almighty God, Creator of all things, sees me as innocent and pure, what is there to strive for? He is already pleased with me.

"You formed my innermost being, shaping my delicate inside and my intricate outside, and wove them all together in my mother's womb. I thank you, God, for making me so mysteriously complex!

Everything you do is marvelously breathtaking. It simply amazes me to think about it! How thoroughly you know me, Lord!"

Psalms 139:13-14 TPT

I have been formed; created in all my complexity by God. I am thoroughly known!

So if He knows me, He can show me who I truly am, and who He has created me to be.

In the Book of Esther, she is facing a difficult task and it says that she was born for "such a time as this". Not only are we formed and made by God but we are also destined for the time in which we live.

It does not mean all things that happen to us are of God or from Him, but it does mean He has all we need to endure and overcome already available to us.

Knowing the truth is the beginning of freedom. Walking in this truth brings the freedom.

Three

Living in pursuit of the "why?"

As the weeks and months went by and my health improved, I began contemplating as to why this had happened and what good could come from it. In wrestling with this, I started to look at careers I could do that would use my experience of what it was like to be a patient.

My desire to be a barrister had not disappeared I just wasn't sure I wanted it as much as I wanted to make use of my "wasted" time.

My Pastor came to visit one day and during the conversation he spoke of how he didn't think that dating a non-Christian was good for me, or right. This infuriated me. How dare he tell me what was right? Enraged, I decided that I would do whatever I wanted and not listen to him.

This was short-lived. Deep down I knew I did not want to marry someone who didn't love God like I did. I wanted to feel connected to someone who I could encourage and who could encourage me to walk with God.

After a few weeks had past I remember having a bad day and my boyfriend got cross and said "How can you believe in a God if He lets you suffer like this?" I'm not totally sure what happened but it was like something snapped inside of me and I said "If you don't understand after 3 years I'm not sure this is going to work". I had ended the relationship. I felt a huge amount of guilt as he had been so kind to me but I was also relieved as I knew it wasn't the best for either of us.

He took it really badly and persisted in contacting me constantly. He phoned every hour for over 24 hours as he was so upset. I was finding this so distressing that my parents suggested I go to visit my sister who was away at university. I stayed with her for a while. I loved this time with her in a new location, one I will always treasure in my heart.

My sister lived with a Pastor and his family. They were amazing part of their community. They ran a church that had a congregation who were predominantly people of African and Jamaican descent. Their house was like Piccadilly Circus, people would wander in looking for food, warmth or a listening ear. No matter what time of day or night they found what they needed. I loved this environment and I knew I would always want my home to be a place of refuge for others too.

On my return, I looked at going back to education but this time chose to study Health and Social Care and Psychology. I really wanted to use my experiences to make a difference.

Getting my brain back into studying took quite an effort and my body was still recovering. I got very tired. The workload was intense but I was intent on completing the course.

With the assignments my perfectionist tendencies raised their head once again. My head lecturer one day commented "You'd hand your work in a brown paper bag with an apology if you could". I knew I had to learn I could only do what I was able to do and that it was good enough.

Throughout my learning I was trying to make sense of the previous three years. Psychology lessons made me question most things. My search for "why" was growing.

Church life was also very different as I had made a move to a larger church with more young people. I wanted good friends and wanted to journey further with Jesus.

I found the youth group quite cliquey but settled all the same. It was great to find a bit more freedom and make new friends, and I loved the worship with a live band.

Being 19 years old, I was very aware of, what Jane Austin would call, "potential suitors". This time I wanted a Christian with the prospect of it being long term. I showed interest and dated a couple of different guys, one out of rebellion as he was a man with a motorbike and the other because he reminded me of a younger Hugh Grant. Two terrible reasons to have a love interest in. Neither were very helpful and they both blew hot and cold in their regard for me. I felt disappointed once again, I felt God was alright but I wasn't sure about His people.

My sister was at university still and I felt very much left behind. People my age were at uni or travelling the world and I was going back to do things I'd missed out on.

It was at this stage in life I realised as a society that we often ask someone what they "do" in order to try to understand them or to give them an identity.

When I was ill and spent most of day in bed, I dreaded seeing anyone who could ask me "what do you do?" How could I answer "nothing"?

I felt that my identity was in my doing and if I answered "nothing" then did that make me "a nothing" as well?

I had started college at 19 years of age with predominantly 16 year olds I really didn't want them to ask why I was only just doing my studies. It was much later in my life that I realised what I was "doing" should not define me.

It's been said that God made us human BE-ings not human DO-ings! This is right! He wants us to BE.

Be with Him.

Be real with Him.

Be like Him.

Be present.

I took a long time in my journey to work this out. His Word says *"It is through him that we live and function and have our identity; just as your own poets have said, 'Our lineage comes from him.'"*

Acts 17:28 TPT

In my search for meaning I was trying to find my identity as well. As a culture we attribute way too much of our identity to our worldly success; education, beauty, finances, popularity.

"for in Him we live and move and have our being.."

Acts 17:28 NKJV

Our true identity is found in Him, and our purpose. Only He can answer the "why's" and I'm not sure we always need to know the answer. I do know that the enemy comes to "steal, kill and destroy", and a lot of the bad stuff we encounter can be attributed to him.

Getting back to my story, I vividly remember saying to God that I loved Him but wasn't sure about His people and that I didn't want to date any more but that I did want His man for me.

In the following few weeks God gave me a verse. I know this can sound strange to some but when it happens you just know. On three separate occasions someone either told me they had this verse for me or I saw it and it appeared to jump off the page at me. On one of these occasions I was staying at someone's house and I awoke in the night and I saw a framed picture on the wall with the very verse in and I knew inside that this was significant. It was *"Delight yourself also in the Lord, And He shall give you the desires of your heart."*

Psalms 37:4 NKJV

I trusted God had heard my prayer and that He would bring me the man He had for me.

Over the summer months my sister returned home and began working for our Dad. She met a guy and quickly began dating him.

One evening they suggested I went with them to Cambridge to get ice cream. My sisters boyfriend said he would invite his brother. I wasn't keen to go on a double date but they persuaded me.

The evening ended up being fun and I met up with him a few more times. He chose to come to church with me and he heard the message and responded. Someone prayed with him to open his heart to Jesus. It was so good. He started a discipleship course with a young man from church and we soon became youth leaders.

At Easter the church had a time away as a retreat. It was my birthday and the speaker got up to preach. He spoke on the very verse ***"Delight yourself also in the Lord, And He shall give you the desires of your heart."***

Psalms 37:4

I felt that God was affirming that I had my prayer answered in this young man. Then before I realised what was happening I was made to go up in front of everyone. I thought they were going to play a joke on me as it was my birthday but instead I found my boyfriend on one knee proposing to me.

Wow I was overjoyed. Finally my life was turning around and surely I had now overcome the worst I could only look forward with excitement.

Four

The Honeymoon Days

The engagement ring had three diamonds, and Jacob said that they represented the two of us with God in the centre. It was a daily reminder sitting pretty upon my hand.

We spent a year planning the wedding and setting up our first home. It was in a beautiful town and was a flint end terrace. It was such a quirky house and I loved it. It was on split levels with a small room (or two) on each of the six floors. The walls were about a foot deep and nothing was level or straight. We renovated it over a number of months to make it ours.

Our garden was open and all our neighbours had a right of way through it. It had a stream running at the bottom and the borders were brimming with old English plants. The following summer was spent with communal garden meet-ups with our wonderfully diverse neighbours. It was so much fun.

Planning a wedding and finishing my college course was exhausting but also exciting. Jacob, my husband-to-be, was also studying as well as working full time so we had our hands full.

The youth group we helped lead at church had loads of young people, and I was the only female leader. The other three were guys who weren't always brilliant with young, emotional girls. We organised lots of different events and ran discipleship groups too.

I had a part time job in a clothes shop and worked mainly

in the men's department. I really enjoyed selling men clothes as they would often let me chose them an outfit. We would be allocated sales targets and I found it much easier to sell to men. This was another environment where my colleagues were guys and often customers wanted a female perspective on how they looked. The job involved a fair amount of banter and it certainly made the hours pass with plenty of laughter.

Jacob and I also had marriage preparation classes which were with two other couples. We were given a cheesy book called The Engaged Couples Handbook which we all read and laughed at. Each week we were guided through different types of adjustments we would encounter; from single-hood to married.

The analogies and stories we were given were hilarious and still a source of amusement today. I remember on the week discussing sexual adjustment, the girls were told that we had to be careful about our closeness and interaction as for the lads it was like a dog wanting it's dinner. If you let the dog smell the food, or taste a little, he would be unstoppable and would just have to devour it. I understood they were trying to help but it was quite archaic and didn't seem to place any responsibility on the man for his reaction. I was also not sure about being described as a dogs dinner!!!

My wedding day came around. I woke very early in the morning and went for a walk as I was both excited and fearful. The morning was spent having hair done and getting ready. Midway through my old Pastor and his wife turned up to take photos. It was a bit unsettling but I thought the motive was good.

My Dad was so lovely to me when he saw me in my dress. It was a perfect moment. He told me how beautiful I looked and how proud he was of me.

The service was beautiful and we had our friends all take a part in it.

The reception was such good fun, with many stories of Jacob's school shenanigans being shared. In the evening we had a jazz band and over two hundred friends and family joined us in the celebration.

We departed around 11.30pm and travelled to our hotel. I was nervous as this would be my very first intimate encounter. It was so very special though as it was as I had always wanted; I had saved myself for my husband.

The following day I attempted to wash the can of hairspray from my hair in the bath. Jacob wandered in dropping something in the tub. I felt around under the water, finding a solitaire diamond ring. He said that the three were now one.

After breakfast we went back to our house to collect our things before going on our mystery honeymoon. Jacob hadn't shared our destination. All I knew was it had to be exotic as I had vaccinations in advance.

Arriving at the airport and being told the time of our flight I hurriedly searched the departure board to discover we were heading to Kenya.

Our honeymoon was incredible. Being together, exploring and revelling in this fabulous new culture. I found a great warmth in the Kenyans we met but found the level of service that other white people expected while showing little respect to them heart-breaking and infuriating.

We went on safari and it was amazing to see the animals in their natural habitat. It was however the people that made me fall in love with the country.

Someone has since said " You can take the girl out of Africa but you can't take the Africa out of the girl". From our honeymoon I always knew a part of my heart came alive there and Africa had a piece of my heart.

Whilst away I became very unwell. I was feverish, vomiting and very lethargic. Unfortunately this triggered another bout of the illness I had endured previously for three years. On return to the UK I just wasn't able to shift the malaise.

Three weeks after our honeymoon we were invited to a family celebration. It was a grand 21st birthday ball. My sister and Jacob's brother were going and we went went with his parents. It was a lavish event but I felt very unwell. I told Jacob but he seemed to only want to stay and party and he sent me home with his parents.

As we were leaving his father realised he had forgotten his camera so returned to the marquee. Once back in the car he said to me "Your husband didn't take long, he is already chatting up someone else, you'll have to keep an eye on him".

I silently wept all the way back to their house and went to bed wondering what on earth I was going to do. This wobble was significantly larger than any before and I felt like my honeymoon was very much over.

Five

"For better, for worse"

Following the party we obviously spoke about what had happened and he reassured me his father was winding me up. He said a girl had flirted with him but it was nothing.

My heart felt unsteady but I prayed about it and sought Gods wisdom to deal with it. I just wanted to forget it had even happened and get back to my idea of what married life would be.

At the weekends we enjoyed updating and decorating our new home as well as hosting friends and family for meals and parties. I still felt really unwell but tried to push through; some days doing better at that than others.

I had enrolled at a local University to study Social Policy in Health (and Psychology). I persisted for a couple of months before this all came crashing down again as my health deteriorated. I was so upset to be back at home in pain and in bed.

The first year of our married life consisted of me being in very poor health and in some ways Jacob tried to be supportive.

He did however, used to joke with his friend that they say in your first year of married life if every time you had sex you'd put a bean in a jar and then the remaining years you would remove a bean every time and that it would work out equal, and if that's the case he would be almost a monk for the rest of his life.

It wasn't how either of us had expected it would be.

This left me feeling I had failed once again by having to give up university and in not being a "good wife".

Instead of seeing these as challenges I saw myself as a failure which is never very productive.

After about a year, as I began to recover, we looked at the next steps we could take. I started volunteering at a hospice back in the town we had originally come from.

We were spending a lot of time travelling to see family and friends there so we soon decided to move back. (Jacob had moved office by then as well so he wasn't even working in the town we currently lived in.)

My work began volunteering in the Education department but I was quickly offered the job as paid employment. They were also setting up a child and adolescent bereavement group and I trained as a group worker. I felt truly alive working with these kids who had already been through so much. Hearing their stories and seeing them work through some of their grief was a huge privilege.

We went back to our previous church and even helped again as youth leaders.

I went to a ladies conference in Bradford with a friend from church. It was an awesome time with God and was such a strengthening encounter. One lady spoke on how she could see a need to reach out to broken women in the UK by having a home they could come to. That they would find hope, love, discipling and freedom from pain that was holding them back. This vision resonated with my heart. I wasn't sure how I could ever be involved as it was so far away but I kept that spark in my heart.

On another note, back at home, Jacob and I decided that as his career was progressing and that my health had improved that we would consider starting a family.

I was also in the process of leaving my paid employment at the hospice to work for a Christian charity providing training.

I fell pregnant straight away and had to tell my new employer on my first day that I would only be able to be there for 7 months or so. This wasn't my finest day and he was very upset and cross. He did come around eventually though.

New families joined the church regularly and we became good friends with a couple who were quite a bit older than us. Stephen was an innovative businessmen and his wife Sara, was an experienced midwife. They were a vibrant couple and we spent a fair amount of time with them.

With Sara being a midwife, I sought her advice and companionship.

The church ran a leadership course and Jacob was asked to attend, as was Sara. It was eight weeks of training in how to be a church leader.

Sara and Stephen were also good friends with my mum and dad, and they loved them very much and they were members of their house group.

The pregnancy went so quickly. Sara had agreed to be my midwife and that helped alleviate some of my anxieties.

During my pregnancy I continued working back at the hospice with the new child and adolescent bereavement project.

I remember coming home one evening after being at the hospice and finding that Jacob had been using pornography. I felt really hurt.

After much arguing I think I realised it had been something that had been going on for a while. I wondered at first if it was since I hadn't been well but it became apparent that it had begun in his teenage years and had become a habit.

It made me feel I wasn't good enough once again. I know that a lot of men in our society see it as normal but I know this isn't how God created it to be. It made it much harder for us to connect intimately as I couldn't stop thinking if he was trying out something he had seen, or even wondered if he was imagining he was with someone else. This was so hard to overcome in my mind and I do think that this causes issues for many couples. The person addicted to porn is also opening their mind to a whole lot of influences as well, as Satan does seek to break down marriages, relationships and genuine connections.

I prayed about it and I remember saying to God "He is Your son deal with him".

This was another wobble I would refuse to fall down from but it was a battle I would have to often fight in my mind.

A month before my due date I was out for dinner at Pizza Hut with Jacob, Stephen and Sara.

There was a heavily pregnant lady on the next table. We joked about us both having cravings for pizza and promptly ordered the same type.

Within half an hour I was having tightenings every few minutes. Sara suggested we went to the hospital just to check everything was okay.

When Sara examined me she announced that I was in established labour. I hadn't got anything with me so I persuaded her to let me go home to get my things.

As we were leaving I saw the lady from Pizza Hut in the labour suite - I thought it must be due to the pizza we both had eaten and should come with a warning on the menu! I really didn't feel ready and I had thought I had another month to prepare. I was apprehensive and excited, but we were going to finally meet our first child.

The labour was fourteen hours long and the end part quite difficult.

As our baby came into the world, I tore. Sara said it was best left and I took her leading.

It was absolutely amazing holding our baby girl. How

could you not thank God in moments like this? She was a true miracle of life. Every part of her tiny and perfectly created. What an amazing God we have.

We named her Sophie, such a beautiful blessing to our lives. We stayed in hospital for three days and were pleased when we got back home. Although we were also a little scared as we didn't know what we were doing.

In the night, after I had fed Sophie, Jacob would wind her and lay her down. We were both so tired and emotional but so delighted with our new addition to our family. We would both just hold her and marvel at her.

My tear however was taking a long time to heal. In the end it was nearly 3 months. My community midwife was horrified that I hadn't had stitches but felt it was too late by the time I saw her. She said she couldn't see why that hadn't been done.

Christmas came around and after having mastitis and my milk turning watery I transitioned to bottle-feeding. This was incredibly difficult as there is a lot of judgement about breast milk being best for baby. Another opportunity for me to feel like I was failing but what could I do?!

Jacob was working hard and it was difficult to find time for us with a new baby. We tried to still socialise with others though and go to church. I remember feeling so very tired.

On New Years' Day we were invited to Stephen and Sara's. It was lovely to get dressed up and go out. A number of guests were there and it was fun to chat and laugh with others. Sophie was happy and I enjoyed introducing her to others. My heart was so full of love for her. I felt like my heart could burst.

Sophie needed her nappy changing so I thought I'd go to the lounge as everyone appeared to be in the kitchen, like all good parties. As I went into the lounge Jacob and Sara were in there and both looked strangely at me as I entered. I wasn't sure why but I proceeded to change Sophie with Sara's help. We enjoyed our time there, only returning home in the early evening.

I was still working with the young peoples bereavement group and now Sophie was on bottled milk I could leave her with Jacob on the Saturdays when I worked. I found it hard to leave her but also felt a responsibility to the young people I had built a level of trust with.

Jacob was working hard during the week and was leaving earlier and earlier. After a broken nights sleep we were both so tired and in the evenings I would long for him to return home to us.

By March I was beginning to be very restless at night. I would have the same nightmare over and over again. In the dream Jacob and Sara would go into her lounge and would be kissing. I would wake up feeling sick.

I would also see them together in our house all over each other, and doing things to each other I would rather not remember. I found it so tormenting. I recall praying and telling God that I was finding it traumatic and to take the dreams away but if it was true to show me more. My dreams became more vivid until one night I awoke and confronted Jacob.

He was totally thrown and tried to deny it at first. With the details I had, and my conviction that God had shown me, he eventually admitted to it. My heart felt totally broken into so many pieces.

I phoned some friends who I knew would pray with me and support me. One of my prayer partners was an elders wife so I knew the church leaders would find out.

My friends were amazing. Offering to pray, help with Sophie and just love me.

However one of the church leaders phoned and said they had heard what had happened and said that it was important I didn't tell anyone else as it could hurt them and make them feel disillusioned with God since Jacob and I were youth leaders. I was devastated and the response was to hush me up and to hide it? It was like taking another punch, after already sustaining quite some damage.

After my previous Pastors' misdemeanours, and now this, I felt very angry. If I hadn't had good godly friends around me I think I would have walked away from church.

I sought God more than ever before. I was also now in a position to decide if I was going to act in the same way the Pastors wife had in my youth, or choose a different way. I had to rely on God for my every breath to keep going and to guide me. I do remember crying most days, a lot of the time, and pouring all my energy into taking care of Sophie.

Was this what was meant by "do you take this man… for better or for worse?"

Six

Facing The Aftermath

The weeks and months that followed seem a bit blurry in my mind, and if truth be told I'm not sure I even want to remember them.

I know Sara reacted very strongly to being found out and both her and Stephen wouldn't have anything to do with me. Sara had said she was very angry that I had "blown things out of proportion" and made it an issue after her being such a good friend. This bewildered me but they also stopped coming to the church which in some ways made life easier; even if I did feel partly responsible for them opting out.

I met up with a friend from church who had experienced something similar and she was extremely supportive. Others however made comments like "Do you not think that something must have been lacking in your marriage otherwise this wouldn't have happened? I know my husband would never do this". (It took some prayer and help from God to forgive that).

Pressing in to God was all I could do to stay sane. He was so faithful and true, and I knew I could trust Him. It also helped that I knew He had already shown me things that were hidden and brought them into the light, so if need be He could do that again.

One day I was crying and praying, "Lord show me if I

should stay or should go, I just want to do what you want?"

The strangest thing happened. The television turned on and it was on the God Channel , which we had never had on Freeview before. Joyce Meyer, a well-known Christian speaker, was on and she said "Someone is wondering right now whether to stay or to go, God wants you to know if you take the Light out of a dark place it just gets darker". I had my answer!

Each situation is unique, and for that time and circumstance, Gods guidance was to stay.

I do think we need to seek God, and His strategy, for all things and at all times, as His way is above ours and it can never be formulated.

A few months after the "great exposure", we received news that Sara had endured a nasty motorbike accident and had broken her leg badly. Jacob looked very concerned and I could see he still had feelings for her. It was hard to see. I was at home and getting on with my daily routine and I strongly sensed God telling me to make dinner for Sara and her family. I knew this was God as I had no earthly desire to do this! I did however do what I felt led to. The next part was going to be harder- I now needed to take it to her. I drove to her house, got the casserole dish and side dishes and walked up the path. She was sat in the garden and looked horrified to see me. I know I said something along the lines of "I'm sorry to hear you've had an accident. God told me to make dinner for you so here it is.." I put it down and left quickly. I got in my car and cried all the way home. I think God was helping me to forgive her and not store hatred or anger in my heart. I won't pretend that it was easy to carry out though, as every part of the hurt "me" did not want to do it.

My prayer partners came over and I told them what God had asked me to do. One of my friends answered with "well

I'd have thrown the casserole at her!" It made us all laugh but we all knew God was doing work on my heart through this.

Jacob seemed sorry but I was hurt. I felt that he was sorry he had been found out, not for what he had actually done. This would become more apparent in years to follow.

We seemed to get on so well in so many ways and we functioned well as a family. The intimacy side was okay but the hurt was quite a barrier for me to fully let my guard down.

Life tried to resume to "normal". Both of us carrying on with our daily routines and planning fun things in the evenings and weekends.

When Sophie was just over a year we decided to try for another baby. This seemed the natural next step for our family. The pregnancy however was very difficult. I was carrying twins but lost one in the first trimester. At 20 weeks I was in established labour and needed to be on bed rest but with a toddler that was tricky. (I did however by the grace of God manage to last right through to 40 weeks).

Being in hospital was hard as I really didn't want to feel this vulnerable and have contact with Sara. I ended up writing to the hospital and asking not to have Sara for personal reasons.

My community midwife mentioned this to me and suggested that what I had been through had happened with others before. I started to think that maybe she had pursued Jacob and that it was just at a time he was feeling vulnerable.

I had a very fast labour and our second daughter, Katie, arrived into our world within 45 minutes. I was desperate to be at home with Sophie as well, so went home within a few hours.

Katie was a fabulous addition to our family. Sophie loved having a baby sister and wanted to take care of her. Katie was a much "livelier" baby, and that's just a kind way of saying she never slept! For the first 18 months she didn't sleep for more than 4 hours at any one time. This season was incredibly difficult.

Sleep deprivation is definitely a method of slow torture.

During this time I was still heading up a parent/carer and baby group at church. This had families attending from local estates, many of whom wouldn't have come into the church normally. We had around 100 children at one point. It was such a privilege and we had craft and story time for the older children, centred around a Bible story. I loved organising events and outreaches through this and made many friendships.

A young mums Bible study group also started up and we spent time seeking after God and pursuing Him. This was a fantastic time of becoming stronger in our relationship with Jesus. I started listening to Christian teachings on the God Channel, and on tape cassettes (remember them?) I even managed to get to some conferences in London and again in Bradford.

One conference I attended with a friend was such an awesome time. It was clear that our understanding of God was deepening but we were in a church that didn't see things the same way which was really hard. We asked if they knew of any churches that believed the same things that they were teaching. The reply was "No, but you will start one!" We both laughed at the absurdity.

In the following years came many challenges and the church didn't seem to like that we believed so fervently in healing and *all* of the spiritual gifts.

I remember being on a course on spiritual gifts and when they didn't cover a number of the gifts and I inquired why. The leader said they were the "exotic gifts not for use here". `I was totally astounded. I asked "What if you have one of these gifts?" and he answered "Then its not for you to use here". The message became loud and clear.

A good friend, who had two small children, also gave

us the news she had stage 4 cancer. We met with her many times for prayer. She saw improvements and always felt the peace and presence of God when we prayed. Even her husband said she should continue to meet us for prayer as he could see the difference in her level of peace. Sadly a couple of elders met with her and told her not to get her hopes up and that we were just over zealous. She ended up torn between what we were sharing with her and what the elders were saying. It was horrible and I hated her feeling this way. We saw her gradually get worse and sadly die. It was after this that we felt God was really telling us that it was time to step out of this church and start a home church. The "absurd" idea came into being.

Seven

The Pursued Became The Pursuer

During this time Jacob was working hard and seeking progression at work as well as being actively involved at church. He had many corporate functions to attend and worked away on occasions. The girls were growing up and life was full.

Over the following years I noticed how flirty Jacob could be and it did concern me.

Many times God spoke to me the verse in Luke 8:17 ***"For nothing is secret that will not be revealed, nor anything hidden that will not be known and come to light."***

This was reassuring and disconcerting. I knew even if I struggled to trust Jacob, because of past events, that I could trust my God. I knew that He had disclosed things to me in the past so they could be brought into the light and dealt with. So I trusted that, if need be, He would do it again. The verse made me think there would be more to come out and I felt apprehensive. Sadly in the years that followed there were many, many occasions where He had to do just that.

There were Christmas parties that got out of hand, and an "accidental" phone call from his mobile meant I heard him discussing it in a drunken taxi ride.

I attended work functions and had ladies strongly hint and share certain indiscretions. I even found out that he had fumbled around and kissed at least two work colleagues, one of which was a young receptionist, who was a Christian herself.

There were friendships' that became more than they should have, with emotional connections that became intimate, and at times obsessive.

The list could go on many times over with more difficult and sordid exploits but the purpose isn't to shame or reveal but to explain that this life hasn't been straightforward and I have experienced much pain. This is not however the only side I wish to tell, as through it all Jesus has walked with me, given me everything I needed to get through each and every time my heart was broken.

It was now obvious that Jacob, who had once been pursued, had now become the pursuer.

Don't get me wrong I know we have an enemy and that he was the one tempting him, but I know Jacob had his part to play too.

Each and every single time I asked God whether it was time for me to leave or to stay. He often reminded me that if you take the light out of a dark place it just gets darker.

On one occasion, in asking for help from a Christian leader, God did say through him that it was my choice. This threw me - yes I was having yet another wobble! I didn't want it to be up to me!

In my discovery however, I realised that God was saying it was okay to stay and try and work through it, and it was okay to go if my heart hurt too much. By this, I understood that God wasn't "holding" me in the situation but that He would back my choice as He knew how much I hurt.

I asked Him to show me how He saw Jacob and He did. From then on I could see the potential within him and the real Jacob that God created him to be. I could see that He was far from free and that his past and stuff that had happened to him was currently defining him and binding him.

Don't misunderstand me, this did not mean that his actions didn't hurt me any more or that I felt obliged to stay, it just meant I saw things from another angle.

God has not called us to modify our behaviour, or to try harder to be good. He knows that in and of ourselves we can't. The old nature, the self driven, self obsessed part of us that wants our rights, our needs and our desires met. This in fact is not the real us. It is the identity we have developed from being born into a corrupt world. We are born disconnected from God, and who we were created to be, because of sin that is in this world. Jesus didn't just come to pay for that sin but to reconnect us to God and to set us free from that old nature. So we can discover who we truly are, without our old man guiding us but allowing God to reveal our true identity.

In Psalm 23 it says in verse 6 ***"Surely your goodness and unfailing love will pursue me all the days of my life, and I will live in the house of the LORD forever."***

When I thought of Jacob as now being the one pursuing these other women it made me feel sick to my stomach. I could easily have taken those actions to mean there was something very wrong with me. If I'm honest at times I did. I had many thoughts that if he loved me, or found me attractive, or wanted to be with me, then he would have been faithful. They were hard to deal with.

God showed me through this verse that He was in fact pursuing me, with His goodness and His unfailing love, and if He thought I was worth loving and chasing after then I did not need to take on those feelings of rejection.

God pursues each one of us as He knows that when we realise who He is and who we truly are then we will have freedom. Freedom to do life with Him. Freedom from sin and selfishness. Free from our past. Free from what others have said or done to us. Free to be the real us.

"Therefore if the Son makes you free, you shall be free indeed."

John 8:36 NKJV

I learnt that I could be free even if others around me were not. I was pursued by God Himself, chased after by His goodness and His outstanding, amazing love. My foundations were secure even in the storms.

Eight

Didn't Come with a Handbook

Parenting books are two a penny but any parent will agree children do not come with a handbook.

Motherhood is something I always looked forward to but I do remember leaving the maternity ward with Sophie and thinking "how am I allowed home with a baby, I have no idea what I'm doing!"

I went to all the parent craft classes. I read books and I had babysat through teenage years. I had even nannied when we were first married, but really parenting is something you learn on your feet in many ways.

Sophie was a contented baby and toddler. She had separation anxiety on going to preschool but I didn't see that as unusual. Sophie was very sensitive and was easily upset. Katie was full of energy and didn't sleep much. She was very confident and independent.

They were both so very different. I loved them equally but I was shocked my children seemed so opposing in their character.

I poured a lot of my energy and focus into loving them and wanting stability for them. I wanted them to have the perfect start in life.

Sophie as a toddler was confident around friends. She loved to sing and dress up.

Katie was very active. If we were at home for any length of time she was like a caged lion, or a human pinball bouncing off the walls. To manage this I had a packed schedule of things to do and places to go - for all our sakes.

When Sophie went to school she was very academic but seemed to hold all her feelings in until I picked her up from school. Upon seeing me she would burst into to tears and seek comfort. Katie was always ahead of her years and wanted to go to school like her sister, and patience wasn't an obvious trait!

Both girls brought so much love into the world and I was privileged to be their mumma.

In her early school years I noticed Sophie had bite marks on her arms and she said Katie had done that. I didn't understand why, but knew Katie had a temper, especially if she felt misunderstood. Trying to deal with these challenges were hard but I navigated them as best I could.

I wanted my children to respect me but not out of fear. I wanted to learn and evolve from how my father had been. I knew he loved me but I didn't want my girls to feel like I had at times.

Sophie became more withdrawn and quiet in her early childhood. Sometimes seeming sad. With her close friends this seemed alleviated by their plays and fun.

Katie was determined and always travelled at a faster pace. She found sitting still to learn more tricky and academia was more of a challenge. She was very sporty and had a very fast working brain that often was innovative as she thought outside of the box.

Katie often tested my patience as she didn't like to take no for an answer. It would cause mass disruption if she didn't get her own way. She seemed to believe that I didn't understand what she wanted or I would have agreed to it.

Sophie liked quiet, calm activities and loved to read and

be alone. Katie liked constant noise, activity and someone to play with.

The girls got involved in most activities around school - swimming, Rainbows, Brownies, learning musical instruments, sports and dance clubs. This meant we were always on a tight schedule and it needed great discipline to run to time almost every day of the week. Sundays were busy with church and most other days had a schedule.

Sophie was kind but seemed to struggle to make close friends at school and clubs. Katie on the other hand found friendships easy to make but harder to maintain, often having fall outs.

Sophie would want birthday parties and to go to discos but not cope with big groups of people. For a number of years she would ask for a birthday party but then when her guests arrived she withdrew to her bedroom refusing to come down!

Katie wanted independence and freedom as soon as possible and struggled to receive guidance or direction. She loved groups of people and parties, and loved the attention. She rarely felt she "needed" her mum.

In early teen years Sophie struggled with fitting in socially. She often spent her lunch times in the library. She had friends but they were quite superficial. With her friends from church and those she had met in her early years was where she seemed more free to be herself.

Jacob loved his girls and wanted to spend weekends with them as he worked such long hours during the week. After working in London for a few years and hardly seeing them he decided to start his own business to help address this. He wanted to be around and watch them grow.

In Sophie's early teen years she flourished academically but her struggles became more apparent. Anxiety levels seemed to be high and generally she was very low in mood.

Katie was a live-wire everywhere except in class where she was described as quiet and reserved. I remember asking the teacher if they had the right child as this did not resemble my experience of Katie at all.

I remember Sophie coming home one day from primary school crying, saying "a boy at school said I'm fat!". I replied "If he said you were a boy would you be crying?" She looked strangely at me and said "No!" I asked why and she explained " Because I know I'm a girl". I said "Then the reason you are crying now is because you believed what he said, and it's really not true".

I think this is a lesson for us all. Words will only truly impact us if we allow them in and consider there to be some truth to them.

Words do have creative power within them but if they are captured and compared to the truth (which is of God) and either judged as truth or lies, then they can only be established with permission. I think we are totally oblivious to this most of the time and therefore their creative power has opportunity to build strongholds in our mind or life.

Sophie took this lie upon herself and it reappeared in her first year of high school. A boy she mistakenly admired called her fat and mocked her in front of other young people and she took it very much to heart. The following three weeks she hardly ate and avoided meal times if she could. She lost a lot of weight very quickly. This was rewarded by many people saying how great she looked and how "well" it made her appear. This became a pattern for a number of years ahead.

By the following year the anxiety levels and depression had really increased.

Katie was seeing her sister go through all of this and found it very hard. She flipped between wanting to help her and wanting to shout at her to shake her out of it. I think I felt the same but managed it a little better as I had the advantage of being an adult, although truth be told sometimes I failed.

We ended up taking her to see a psychiatrist after therapy had not really helped. Things began to spiral and over the next few months it got much worse.

During this time my father was very unwell with cancer and I spent a lot of time looking after him and Sophie. He was very good with her and showed her much love. We would spend time a couple of days a week visiting him, or him us. He would often talk to Sophie and tell me to go do something as they wanted to chat.

The times I spent alone with him, he spoke such affirming words over who I had become and the call he felt was on my life. He was so keen for me to continue speaking in church, and doing work in Africa. This was interspersed with his dissection on other topics which he always had strong opinions on.

I remember him telling me that he valued my quiet strength - he even called me his "rock". This assured me our relationship had drastically changed, as had he. He had become my biggest encourager, something I had not thought possible.

Sadly after many months of helping to care for him he died. I was so upset, I had really thought we would have seen him healed. We had seen it in the past.

He had been given a diagnosis 7 years previously and we had seen the cancer retreat after prayer.

I had many unanswered questions but I did know he was tired of standing and fighting against it, and I think I had gotten tired too.

Mum came to stay for the week after Dad died. We then had the work of sorting his estate, which he had made slightly easier by putting things in order.

Following his death Sophie hit a new low. She took it very hard. Within two weeks of him dying she became quite suicidal and greater intervention was sought. Life was so tough.

I didn't remember reading about any of these complications in my parenting handbooks and I felt very much out of my depth. I did trust that God would make a way through and I knew I needed His help - now more than ever.

Nine

Clinging on

Trigger warning

After a number of suicide attempts and a flurry of self-harm, Sophie just seemed to be getting worse.

Just before her birthday she attended an appointment with her therapist. We were advised they were extremely concerned for her welfare and thought she needed in-patient care.

The following day we took her to a psychiatric hospital over an hour from our home. I sat in the back of the car with Katie one side of Sophie, and me on the other, holding her hand as she sat staring out of the window, looking numb.

My heart was breaking and I could see Katies' and Jacobs' was too. Sophie did not go in willingly or quietly, she was very resistant. After spending a number of hours there, we made the journey home in silence. Everyone wiping away their tears while staring at the passing countryside.

Many weeks, months and events followed. I am keeping this brief for my own sanity as well as yours. The ward was not particularly "safe". There were riots, fights, injuries and many restraints. Things were not improving and Sophie was not communicating. She refused to eat on many occasions and would harm herself repeatedly. I visited every evening for a couple of hours.

One particular evening we received a phone call to say that Sophie had escaped and the police had been looking for her and others for over an hour. I have never felt so sick in all my life. The only thing I could do was to pray. It was the best thing I could do, but I felt very shut down emotionally. After another hour, Sophie called from a random number. She told me where she was and I informed the police. She had tried to jump from a bridge but another patient had persuaded her not to - I will forever be grateful to God and this amazing young lady for saving her.

In that same year just after Christmas we were informed that Sophie had experienced a flashback and was very distressed. They told us that they thought she had been assaulted in the past and asked us questions. Sophie did not remember the flashback but was able to tell us someone that we knew well had sexually assaulted her. The staff told us that they were sure she had experienced another assault over a longer period of time and certain details. When they told her what she had said, she cried as she remembered certain events.

Her brain had been trying to protect her from the pain by shutting the memories out, but her body and her unconscious mind were well aware and exhibiting a trauma response.

Shortly after this revelation Sophie had an incident whereby she had a ligature around her neck and needed emergency care. We were informed and we rushed to the hospital. High alert was a new way of life for us. Feeling nauseous and high vigilance were the status quo. These emergencies happened far too regularly.

We arrived at the hospital to find out that she was still in resuscitation. They were unsure if there was any brain damage encountered or whether she would regain consciousness. The only thing to do was seek God and pray. We sat in a side room sobbing and praying. I remembered that God had told me before she was born that she would be a bringer of Good News. I spoke out that that hadn't happened yet so this could not be the end of her story. Miraculously within a few hours she recovered, and she returned to the psychiatric hospital.

A few days following this incident, the hospital informed us that she was moving to a more secure ward two hundred and forty miles away. This was devastating. We understood the concern but how were we to function as a family with this much distance between us?

Sophie really didn't want to be that far away from me. She refused to eat and within three weeks of arriving, and many emergency interventions, she was hospitalised for tube feeding.

Sophie required twenty four hour one-to-one support to help keep her safe. It should have really been two-to-one but the hospital didn't have staff to allow for this. I ended up staying for a couple of weeks as I was so concerned for her safety.

While in this general hospital. Sophie had a wonderful nurse who went over and above to connect with her and understand what she was going through. She even shared some personal experience to help Sophie. This was the first time in five months there seemed to be any signs of improvement. Sophie told this nurse what she had gone through (well, at least the parts her brain allowed her to know at this point!) Sophie began to want, or want to want, to get better.

The hospital transferred her to an eating disorder secure ward near London. This was nearer home but still an hour and a half away.

The new hospital was amazing. The consultant was fabulous. He spoke to Sophie with such care and concern. He was very strict with boundaries but really listened to her, and also to me. This was a new experience for us both as previous psychiatrists had very much told us their opinions without listening to us.

Within the first couple of weeks of Sophie being there I received a phone call informing me that Sophie had experienced another flashback whereby she had given enough details to inform the staff of abuse. They phoned the police and called me to come immediately. I was met by a member of staff who asked me questions and told me that Sophie was not yet aware that they had informed police.

I went to see Sophie and had the unenviable task of telling her the police had also arrived. She was petrified and sobbed and sobbed.

Sophie did manage to speak to the police but was very distressed. This interview was just the beginning.

The period of time with police intervention carried on for a number of months. The "family friend" was picked up by police and questioned and so was his wife. Evidence was taken but sadly it was not fully investigated as they felt that it would not get through court - partly because of how poorly Sophie still was. The other person who had abused her had physically and sexually abused her and she was extremely frightened of the repercussions. He had threatened Sophie that he would go after Katie if she ever told anyone and this remained a huge fear to her. In the end Sophie agreed to drop the case due to the fear, stress and the inactivity in the other case.

Despite this Sophie had improved a great deal and she was finally discharged home.

Months of adapting to life at home were Sophie's next challenge. It was far from linear. In fact for the next few years it was very up and down.

Sophie stayed in contact with a girl she had been in hospital with while "up north". They would write to each other frequently. This young lady had many challenges herself and sadly she ended up taking her own life. This threw Sophie into a spiral once again. More hospital admissions and distressing times followed.

This next hospital was an adult in-patient ward which was on a totally different level of "unwell" patients. The consultants were also an all-time low too. Both consultants caused significant harm to Sophie and to our family. One was verbally and physically abusive (believe it or not!) The other sowed horrendous doubts as to whether I was the issue behind all of Sophies' distress. (This was in response to my challenging his opinion on whether Sophie was safe enough to come home.)

As a family we had been fighting "the system" to get help for Sophie for a number of years and we had always confronted any issues. This time it was one hell of a fight. I would never normally use that phrase but it was like encountering satan himself.

Sophie was told by the consultant and his team that I was controlling and that she could have independence from me. They agreed to place her in independent living and informed me of this in a meeting where Sophie and I faced thirteen professionals. This was hard enough for me to deal with let alone Sophie.

I felt utterly broken.

I remember praying that only God could vindicate me and protect Sophie, I wasn't sure what else I could do as everyone agreed to this new pathway forward.

Eventually Sophie was placed at a supported living accommodation that was super helpful to her. Within a few weeks and months the staff soon realised that Sophie got a lot of encouragement and support from me. They did not believe that I was the issue and they began to include me in her care planning. She found a good local church and found a few very loving companions.

After two years Sophie moved out into her own flat. Her

journey was still a mountainous one but she kept moving in the general direction of up.

More disclosures came out, and the main issues from abuse hit us all hard. It is so hard to explain to those that have not experienced the devastation that these things cause. The destruction it does to the soul of the victim, and those that love them.

(So many incidents and battles were encountered that this is in fact a brief summary. Many have been left out due to the triggering nature and it is not necessary for us to relive them. It's safe to say it was a challenging time).

Betrayal, guilt, anger and shock are just a few emotions that came in waves. God was so faithful in helping with each and every wave of emotion. If we took these emotions to Him, He faithfully guided us through each wave, ensuring we didn't drown.

How did we hold on? I'm not totally sure. I do know without God I would probably have been a nervous wreck at best, or a psych patient myself at worse.

Not all days have been pretty, faith-filled or victorious. We can say with confidence though, that with Gods help we did cling on. Sophie more than most, even if only by her fingertips.

Ten

Katie

Throughout Katie's life she had always been a bundle of energy, and we loved her for it, albeit parenting at times was exhausting!

From early teens she took on the big sister role, even though she was the youngest. At school people would tell her when Sophie was crying and she felt responsible for keeping an eye on her sister. Katie knew Sophie was emotional and determined to be a fixer and to "stay strong". She developed a reputation as someone not to be messed with. I think she did this as she felt she needed to be the protector.

Katie always has had the biggest heart.

Many years ago we travelled to Wales to climb Snowdon. On the descent Katie seemed to be slowing a little but due to her young age I just assumed that to be normal. When we eventually got back to the car, after a number of hours, I reached to take her rucksack to place in the car. Her bag was exceptionally heavy. I queried as to what on earth was in the bag. Katie had decided that collecting slate from the mountain in order to sell them would raise vital funds for orphan children in Africa. We didn't have the heart to tell her that it was totally illegal!

This was only one of many ways in which Katie tried to raise money for others. I remember her making many loom band bracelets and taking them to church. Her sales method was to ask how many each person would like to buy, for one pound each, and if someone replied that they would have one she would reply with "One? They are for orphans!!" Nothing like a bit of guilt-tripping people into giving?!

Where Sophie began to get more and more unwell this obviously effected Katie too. She wanted to fix things and make everything better but she, like us, struggled to find an answer.

Katie would always try to encourage Sophie that she was loved and that things were going to be okay, but frustration would sometimes overwhelm her and she would get cross. These outbursts were understandable but confusing for Sophie. They would both feel guilty. Sophie for being the way she was and seeing how it effected Katie, and Katie for exploding and upsetting her sister.

When I had to travel to see Sophie in hospital Katie found it very hard with me being away. She obviously also struggled with what her sister was going through. For her, trying to function "normally" at school, and dealing with the every day challenges of puberty was incredibly hard with everything else going on . I would spend time each evening talking to her on the phone but I knew she was feeling like I wasn't there for her when she needed me. This has taken years to overcome. Katie can see in hindsight I had no other option, but to her in those moments she felt so alone. I constantly felt torn between wanting to help both of my girls and it was torturous not to be able to be with both of them when they needed me.

During these years Katie had moments of rebellion. I totally understood, it was her trying to make herself feel better. One such incident, I remember returning home after visiting Sophie, to find Katie and her friend had drunk A LOT of alcohol. They both proceeded to "re-decorate" most of the upstairs of our house. They even filled their own school bags with vomit!!!!

In light of everything else going on this wasn't a drama. It wasn't ideal, it wasn't what I wanted but in comparison this felt like normal teenage rebellion.

School noticed that Katie was feeling anxious and concentrating on her studies wasn't easy for her. They were very good at making allowances for her.

Throughout the years of Sophie's challenges, Katie sought close friends and boyfriends to bring a distraction and a distance between her family situation and her daily life. She got into clubbing and partying early and at times connected with people that weren't always good for her. This brought troubles of their own and Katie at times felt so overwhelmed with her circumstances that she too felt like she couldn't cope and made impulsive choices. As parents we hated seeing her making these choices and were constantly aware that we were walking a very difficult tight rope.

Katie chose to move out of home at 17 years of age and I hated the distance between us. I stayed in close contact with her and when things started to go really wrong she would call in distress. I knew that when the girls were young I always told them that if they ever made bad decisions and wanted to get out of the situation that they were to call me and I would without judgement help however i could. I must admit I needed Katie to know that on a number of occasions and I was relieved she did just that.

The anxiety and insomnia that Katie lived with carried on for many years and became almost the status quo. She has always been incredibly resilient with everything that she has experienced and we have always been so proud of her.

She achieved all of her GCSE's, college diploma and worked a number of jobs. Even through Covid-19 she managed to turn that time which was so constraining around. She spent time making new friends (and even boyfriend) online, learned new skills and sought work experience which led her into a new career path.

This wasn't plain sailing for her either. Unfortunately she had a boss who made sexually inappropriate comments to her over a prolonged period until she became too scared to go into work. She dealt with it professionally and took it through the correct channels but ended up feeling unable to stay working for this company. At the time it felt like another large loss as she loved the job.

We prayed that God would guide her to the right job and repay what had been stolen. This was answered in such a huge way. She has a wonderful job and a boss that is so different and so considerate it is obvious this is a God provision.

Katie has embraced adulthood in an amazing way. She is working a full-time job, running her own home and maintaining friendships and her relationships in the most stable way.

She has continued to have challenges come her way but we are closer than ever and have a lovely friendship and mother-daughter connection, and we continue to pray and see God guide us.

Eleven

Forgiveness

Many people have written books on this subject, or whole teaching series, so I'm not going to fully address this vast subject. I will simply enlighten you to the journey I am on.

As you have read in this book, I have had a few weighty issues that have happened in my life, along with many more minor ones too.

I am aware we all have a mixture of stresses and strains through life, many of which are a result of other peoples' behaviours. This presents us with the conundrum of what to do with those feelings and thoughts we have towards those that have harmed us.

The Bible tells us to forgive others and especially in light of how much we have been forgiven.

Jesus taught His disciples to pray:

And forgive us our debts, as we have forgiven our debtors [letting go of both the wrong and the resentment]."

Matthew 6:12 AMP

It shows that as we need forgiveness, we also need to offer it. I like this translation, as it describes what forgiveness is; "letting go of both the wrong and the resentment".

When Mary Magdalene washed and anointed Jesus' feet, He explained to Simon this was her response to knowing how much she had been forgiven.

> *"Then he turned to the woman and said to Simon, "Look at this woman kneeling here. When I entered your home, you didn't offer me water to wash the dust from my feet, but she has washed them with her tears and wiped them with her hair. You didn't greet me with a kiss, but from the time I first came in, she has not stopped kissing my feet. You neglected the courtesy of olive oil to anoint my head, but she has anointed my feet with rare perfume. "I tell you, her sins—and they are many—have been forgiven, so she has shown me much love. But a person who is forgiven little shows only little love." Then Jesus said to the woman, "Your sins are forgiven.""*
>
> **Luke 7:44-48 NLT**

Our response to His forgiveness is shown by our love towards Him. If we realise how much He has done for us we will love Him so much more. I think this requires us to accurately judge our own condition before His intervention. It demands true humility. Jesus also asks us to show love through having forgiveness for others'.

This can sound easy until you have been seriously hurt by another person. It is true, but how do we do this? And, is it a one-time fixes all?

I know I have much to learn still but I can share my insights, and I'm not trying to be glib as I know it can be a challenge.

What I have learned so far is that forgiveness is about releasing those feelings of hurt and any bitterness that you have, and giving them to God. It is saying I don't want to hold on to these feelings and thoughts any more. I give that person, those events and even the thoughts and feelings I have about the situation to You, God, to deal with.

The process of forgiveness for me has often come in layers. I have thought I have released it all to God but He shows me aspects of the hurt that I have continued to harbour in my heart, usually when I'm ready to deal with a bit more "heart surgery".

I have found forgiveness to be like an onion. It has many layers and often involves tears!

It can in some instances involve talking to the person involved but on other occasions it definitely has not. In some of the situations I could not have addressed it directly with the person involved or it wouldn't have been safe for either myself or my daughter.

If the offender has not shown any sign of genuine sorrow for the pain caused, I think I have found it harder to let go of. In these circumstances full reconciliation is then not found but forgiveness still can be.

Forgiveness is something between us and God, and is irrelevant how the offending party feels. (Reconciliation however does require something more.)

Forgiveness sets <u>us</u> free from hatred and bitterness. These destructive emotions can eat away at us and allow the pain to fester, grow and bring in a whole array of other harmful things such as mental and physical sickness. Simply put, forgiveness is good for us!

Our hearts need to be pure and set apart for God, not holding onto grudges which only brings hardness and darkness.

In Proverbs it tells us:

"Guard your heart above all else, for it determines the course of your life."

Proverbs 4:23 NLT

It makes it clear that our life's direction is dependant upon us keeping our hearts in check and not allowing it to become hard.

In Philippians it tells us to bring everything to God in prayer:

"Do not be anxious or worried about anything, but in everything [every circumstance and situation] by prayer and petition with thanksgiving, continue to make your [specific] requests known to God. And the peace of God [that peace which reassures the heart, that peace] which transcends all understanding, [that peace which] stands guard over your hearts and your minds in Christ Jesus [is yours]."

Philippians 4:6-7 AMP

If we bring every part of our life to Him, He is faithful and just and will show us the way forward.

"Trust in the Lord with all your heart, And lean not on your own understanding; In all your ways acknowledge Him, And He shall direct your paths."

Proverbs 3:5-6 NKJV

"In all your ways acknowledge Him" means to do things His way not our own. So if He says forgive, then that is what I know I want to do. He promises that as a result He will guide my journey forward.

What forgiveness is NOT

Forgiveness is not without boundaries. It does not mean that you allow people to continue to harm you. I think in churches we have often times told people to forgive no matter what, which is true. But, we have not told people that they don't have stay in abusive situations. This has led to many Christians suffering unnecessarily for years thinking that this is what God is requiring of them.

It also does not mean you put boundaries up in a way that means you react as if you expect everyone to hurt you.

Forgiveness is a peacemaker within us. It helps us find freedom from resentment and pain. Forgiveness is also a teacher, helping us to guard against those situations in the future, wherever possible, but does not allow us to harden ourselves to everyone either. Our hearts need to stay sensitive to God and others.

In the situation with my husband and friend having an affair, God guided me to take the home-cooked meal as a way of me "letting go" and acting on it. The friendship however was never restored. She never admitted to doing anything wrong and it wasn't helpful for my husband and I to remain in contact with her.

Reconciliation and repentance

Reconciliation is possible when we have shown forgiveness towards the person who has hurt us and there has been repentance on their part for the hurt caused. Trust is then built over time, where the *fruit of repentance* is shown.

Just because you have forgiven someone and they have said sorry does not mean things automatically return to where they were before.

Repentance actually means to have godly sorrow that leads to a person wanting to totally turn away from the direction they were going or what they were doing. It is this type of sorrow that produces change in a person. This doesn't mean they will be perfect at all times but it means their heart strongly desires not to be doing those things any more, and their actions show that. This is the fruit of their repentance.

When we repent and take our weaknesses to God, He shows us who He has created us to be and when we receive new life in Him, He makes us that brand new person. It is only when we truly know who we are, and die to our old self that we see lasting change. This repentance brings freedom.

When we do things out of our old nature and need to repent, it is only through taking it to Jesus, saying sorry and thanking Him that this isn't who we are any more, that we are truly transformed. It is in letting it go and letting God deal with it, and us!

More than anything I want my heart to be sensitive to God, and to acknowledge Him and His ways in all I do. I want His Holy Spirit to be free to perform what ever heart surgery I require. If there are dark places in my heart I want them removed. I want a heart that is sensitive to those around me and I want to love like Jesus.

I know that this does not involve me becoming a "doormat" and does not leave me unprotected and open to abuse - although that may still come my way.

I trust that God is my Protector. Holy Spirit guides me into all truth and shows me things to come. He gives me discernment and helps me at all times. Jesus has shown me more forgiveness than I will ever need to extend and He is gentle and kind as He guides me through any process of letting go and having forgiveness for another human being. This is my journey and I hope it helps you on your journey of forgiveness.

Twelve

Freedom

I mentioned in the previous chapter that both forgiveness and repentance bring freedom, and they do.

Freedom is often understood as being able to choose or act without constraint. This is not biblical freedom.

We were created to walk and talk with God; Father, Son and Holy Spirit. When Adam and Eve used their freedom to side with the enemy our freedom was lost. God had given us authority on the earth and in the Garden that was shared with the enemy.

Satan never has and never will play fair. He has spend thousands of years using that authority to steal, kill and destroy humankind.

The Father sent Jesus to earth to get that authority back and to set us free from the enemies' hold over us.

True biblical freedom is receiving this freedom and enforcing it.

It is not about living without constraint at all , but it is living within the boundaries God has placed for our ultimate well-being.

It's freedom to walk and talk with Him again.
It's freedom to find our true self, which is only found in Him.
It's freedom from sin and its effects.
It's freedom from the power of the enemy.

In John 8:32 it says that *"**you shall know the truth and the truth shall make you free**"* (NKJV). In The Passion Translation it *says ""**Jesus said to those Jews who believed in him, "When you continue to embrace all that I teach, you prove that you are my true followers. For if you embrace the truth, it will release true freedom into your lives."""***

Knowing and embracing the truth brings freedom. Jesus taught us so many things on how to live free. The bible speaks about how we must keep hold of it.

*"**It was for this freedom that Christ set us free [completely liberating us]; therefore keep standing firm and do not be subject again to a yoke of slavery [which you once removed]."***

Galatians 5:1 AMP

Circumstances of life can cause us so much pain, distress and trauma that the enemy uses it to hold us and to bind us. Some times it can be from our own choices, and others times it is from choices that other people make and inflict upon us.

We could see the pain that Sophie was carrying and weren't aware of where this had come from.

In the big picture we can see that people made choices that inflicted great pain upon her.

The enemy used these broken people to cause more brokenness.

It is like a snowball rolling down a snowy hill gaining momentum and gaining in size. As time passes more pain is experienced by more people… it "snowballs"!

Jesus came to put an end to this. He has given the power and authority back to us so we can break the cycle and to obliterate the snowball.

For years we prayed for Sophie. We were asking why and how we could "fix" it.

One Easter, Sophie got to the point again where she felt she couldn't carry the pain and torment she felt inside any longer. Some good friends and I spent a few hours in prayer with her asking Holy Spirit to show us His way through.

He revealed to Sophie more of what she had experienced that had been trapped in a part of her brain, and He showed us that spiritually she was being oppressed. She needed deliverance.

In the months that followed God showed me Sophie was like a country that had an enemy illegally occupying some of the land. Deliverance was the country, or its allies, using its legal powers to evict the enemy out of that land. So we did just that.

The Bible says ***"how God anointed Jesus of Nazareth with the Holy Spirit and with great power; and He went around doing good and healing all who were oppressed by the devil, because God was with Him."***

Acts 10:38 AMP

We are followers of Jesus; we get to do what He did and is doing.

What did this look like? Well we prayed in tongues and called out whatever He guided us to say.

This was the beginning of this deliverance journey for Sophie. Later that year we attended a conference at a church who have a very well-established deliverance ministry where she received much more. She was finally free!

How has this looked in the past year or so? Well, Sophie is now free and she knows it. It has been clear for all to see. Especially those who have walked this arduous journey with her.

Does she have wobbles or times where things come up? Absolutely! Her old way of thinking and the enemy haven't given up their last-ditch attempts just yet.

However, our explanation is this: she is free and is now learning to walk in that freedom!

I can not tell you how much this is the chapter I longed to write from the beginning of this book!

This freedom is something I have also received and a journey I'm travelling. The perfectionism, past hurts, traumas and things that would seek to hold me back. But a life that seeks to overcome and walk in freedom is the only life I desire. It can be hard getting to that new way of thinking and living but it's definitely the only way forward.

Katie has found some freedom and Jacob too, which is wonderful. I'm. We are all on our own journey!

Is this a neat little ending to a difficult tale? No. It is incomplete. It is unfinished and I can't guarantee more challenges won't be faced. But, what I can be sure of is that freedom is available. It is worth seeking and it can be found and learned to walk in.

Once you kick an enemy out of occupied land they often try at intermittent times to recapture the land. Becoming a law-enforcer of what Jesus came to give us is required.

Knowing this is the enemies strategy means we must remain vigilant. The more you resist the sooner he will give up with that avenue of attack.

Old ways of thinking and mind-games have to be resisted.

With time the new way of thinking, and the strength gained from these challenges, only weakens the advances.

Holy Spirit brings freedom. If ever I feel under attack or like I'm struggling I know that reminding myself of the truth and praying in tongues builds me up.

> **"For the Lord is the Spirit, and wherever the Spirit of the Lord is, there is freedom."**
>
> **2 Corinthians 3:17 NLT**

Whatever you face, allow Holy Spirit to bring freedom, wisdom and to guide you.

Pray in tongues.

Praying in the Spirit is a great way of getting out of your own way of thinking and giving Him room. He will speak to you, build you up and strengthen you.

If you pray for something, whether it is a sickness, situation or any kind of challenge, if it is resistant to change, it is worth asking Holy Spirit if deliverance is needed. He will show you what to do or help guide you to someone who can help.

I urge you not to leave things without finding assistance from others who can help you find freedom. This freedom may come through finding forgiveness, repentance, reconciliation, ultimately receiving Jesus as your Lord or deliverance. Freedom is worth going after!

Thirteen

Restoration

Restoration can be described as repairing, reinstating, rehabilitating, rebuilding, mending or reconditioning something or someone back to a good condition.

Jesus came to restore the broken relationship we had with the Father, to reinstate the level of intimacy and companionship He had always intended. He also came to mend the effects of this broken down relationship and the influence and effects of the enemy.

Jesus quoted from Isaiah, when He said *""The Spirit of the Lord is upon me, for he has anointed me to bring Good News to the poor. He has sent me to proclaim that captives will be released, that the blind will see, that the oppressed will be set free, and that the time of the Lord's favor has come. ""*

Luke 4:18–19 NLT

Restoration and freedom is what Gods' desire has always been. His original intention for His children.

Even in the Old Testament God instituted a time of restoring all (returning even more than before):

"And you shall consecrate the fiftieth year and proclaim freedom [for the slaves] throughout the

land to all its inhabitants. It shall be a Jubilee (year of remission) for you, and each of you shall return to his own [ancestral] property [that was sold to another because of poverty], and each of you shall return to his family [from whom he was separated by bondage]."

Leviticus 25:10 AMP

In Job 42 it says in verse 10, *""And the Lord restored Job's losses when he prayed for his friends. Indeed the Lord gave Job twice as much as he had before."*

Job 42:10 NKJV

Intended restoration is painted throughout the whole of the Bible following the fall of man.

In God's economy if much has been taken, stolen or lost, then what is restored is far greater than what was there in the first place.

We have been created in three parts, just like God. We are spirit, soul (mind, will and emotions) and body. Jesus came to provide restoration for every part of us.

This is GOOD NEWS!

Our experience isn't a one-stop shop but a continual restoration process. We are seeing God restore so much within our family and our lives and we know there is so much more to come. God is so good.

When you open a messy desk drawer you have to empty it out to clean and tidy it up. This is what the restoration process can feel like. I think my desk has a number of drawers and together Jesus, Holy Spirit and Father are helping me open and go through each one as I'm ready to help deal with them.

I know and trust that He is also doing that with Jacob, Sophie and Katie.

He wants to do that for you too.

Fourteen

Will the Real April Please Stand Up?

In chapter one I spoke of how we all have hearts that long to be understood and known. This does require us to know who we are first of all.

Circumstances, experiences and how we have been described or treated can define us. Allowing this is very dangerous though, as these are constantly changing.

Even our own perceptions of who we are have been built upon years of these things, so how can we know who we truly are?

The Bible is a good place to start. There are so many truths written in there about who God has created us to be. Holy Spirit wants to bring that alive in our hearts and minds, and to take us on a journey of discovery.

This process is about letting go of all of the preconceived ideas we have long held and even those things others have said that we have harboured in our inner being. It is in changing how we view ourselves by letting that go and embracing what God says.

This in itself will bring so much freedom and restoration. It will also guide you in finding the answer to the question "What am I here for? What is my purpose on earth?"

Imagine running a marathon to get to the end of it and realise you have run in the wrong direction and in the wrong lane.

I know I don't want to get to the end of my life and God to tell me or show me all the things I've missed out on or that I didn't complete because I'd not sought to follow His plan.

> ***"For I know the plans I have for you," says the Lord. "They are plans for good and not for disaster, to give you a future and a hope."***
>
> **Jeremiah 29:11 NLT**

I want His good plans, His future which is filled with hope.

In fact God has shown me my hearts' passion is to be a bringer of hope to others. If this wasn't the case I don't think this book would have been completed. Many times I have wanted to delete it, but I know He has told me it will help others find hope and freedom.

My true identity is wrapped up in Jesus. I want to be who He has created me to be and to fulfil the adventures He has set aside for me.

I hope this ignites a desire in you to chase after your unique identity and plan that God has placed within you too.

Fifteen

Journey Not Destination

Like I said this book isn't one with a neatly packaged happy ending. I know the ending is a happy one but it is still to be played out.

Do I know what that looks like? Not really!

What I do know is that I'm on a journey with the best travel companions and guides ever! Father, Jesus and Holy Spirit know the best routes, best sights to see and adventures to partake in. They have divine appointments lined up and I don't want to miss any of it.

Will there be more drawers to empty out, to be cleaned and tidied? Yes, undoubtedly. Will every day be a "joy"? We shall see. But I know that this journey is one which I wouldn't miss for anything.

Even if there are some moments I'll be tempted to wobble I know I'll be okay, because "Weebles wobble but they down fall down".